The weather was very cold in January. There was snow all over the ground. There was ice all over the pond. The ducks were all going head over heels.

Kevin and Lotty went to the pond to slide on the ice. Kevin was the first to tread on the ice. Oops! He slid along with his legs spread out.

Lotty was the next to have a go. Oops! Her legs spread out so much that she was sliding on her tummy. She went round and round in a spin.

Wellington went to the pond to join Kevin and Lotty. He tried to tread on the ice carefully. Oops! He went head over heels just like the ducks.

Kevin wanted to know who could slide the furthest. He and Lotty lined up at the edge of the pond.

"Ready, steady, go," barked Wellington.

Kevin and Lotty slid along the ice. Oh no! ... The ice was very thin in the middle of the pond. ... CRACK ... Kevin fell in the icy water. His head went under the ice.

Splash! Lotty fell in after him. The water was freezing! The two dogs came up and took a deep breath. Then they tried to get back on to the ice.

BUT ... The ice cracked again ... and again. Kevin and Lotty could not get back on it. Their heads kept going under the freezing water.

Meanwhile, Wellington was thinking about what to do. He leapt on to the ice, ... and ... because he was heavy, he cracked it too. He pushed his way through the ice to meet Kevin and Lotty.

Wellington took Kevin and Lotty back to the bank. They crawled on to the snowy grass feeling very, very cold. They were glad to be out of the icy water. They would not tread on thin ice again.

"ea"

head   tread

spread   ready

steady   heavy

leapt   breath

weather